chinese
vegetarian

chinese vegetarian

Editor: Lydia Leong
Designer: Benson Tan
Series Designer: Bernard Go Kwang Meng

This book contains previously published material from Contemporary Chinese Vegetarian Cuisine

Copyright © 2008 Marshall Cavendish International (Asia) Private Limited
Reprinted 2009

Published by Marshall Cavendish Cuisine
An imprint of Marshall Cavendish International
1 New Industrial Road, Singapore 536196

All rights reserved

No part of this publication may be reproduced, stored in a retrieval system or transmitted, in any form or by any means, electronic, mechanical, photocopying, recording or otherwise, without the prior permission of the copyright owner. Request for permission should be addressed to the Publisher, Marshall Cavendish International (Asia) Private Limited, 1 New Industrial Road, Singapore 536196. Tel: (65) 6213 9300, Fax: (65) 6285 4871.
E-mail: te@sg.marshallcavendish.com

Limits of Liability/Disclaimer of Warranty: The Author and Publisher of this book have used their best efforts in preparing this book. The Publisher makes no representation or warranties with respect to the contents of this book and is not responsible for the outcome of any recipe in this book. While the Publisher has reviewed each recipe carefully, the reader may not always achieve the results desired due to variations in ingredients, cooking temperatures and individual cooking abilities. The Publisher shall in no event be liable for any loss of profit or any other commercial damage, including but not limited to special, incidental, consequential, or other damages.

Other Marshall Cavendish Offices:
Marshall Cavendish Ltd.5th Floor, 32-38 Saffron Hill, London EC1N 8FH • Marshall Cavendish Corporation. 99 White Plains Road, Tarrytown NY 10591-9001, USA • Marshall Cavendish International (Thailand) Co Ltd. 253 Asoke, 12th Flr, Sukhumvit 21 Road, Klongtoey Nua, Wattana, Bangkok 10110, Thailand • Marshall Cavendish (Malaysia) Sdn Bhd, Times Subang, Lot 46, Subang Hi-Tech Industrial Park, Batu Tiga, 40000 Shah Alam, Selangor Darul Ehsan, Malaysia

Marshall Cavendish is a trademark of Times Publishing Limited

National Library Board Singapore Cataloguing in Publication Data

Chinese vegetarian. - Singapore : Marshall Cavendish Cuisine, c2008
p. cm. – (Mini cookbooks)
"This book contains previously published material from Contemporary Chinese vegetarian cuisine"--T.p. verso.
ISBN-13 : 978-981-261-539-8
ISBN-10 : 981-261-539-3

1. Vegetarian cookery. 2. Cookery, Chinese. I. Title: Contemporary Chinese vegetarian cuisine. II. Series: Mini cookbooks

TX837
641.5636 -- dc22   OCN179730137

Printed in Singapore by Saik Wah Press Pte Ltd

contents

soup of dough slices 10

family pot 12

hot and sour soup 14

vegetarian shark's fin soup 16

pot of prosperity 18

soup of assorted shreds 21

shredded bean curd soup 22

cucumbers with mung bean sheets 25

bean curd skin with black sesame seeds 26

simple fried rice 29

vegetarian glutinous rice 30

stir-fried vermicelli 33

pekinese noodles in special sauce 34
fried mouse-tail noodles 36
shanghainese fried rice cakes 39
golden mushrooms with grated ginger 40
stuffed chinese mushrooms 42
chinese mushrooms with braised chestnuts 45
abalone mushrooms in sweet-sour sauce 46
vegetables with bean curd knots 49
water chestnuts in black bean sauce 50
bean cake strips with french beans 53
stuffed cucumber 54
stuffed bitter gourd 56

bean curd strips with chinese chives 59
bean curd rolls with basil 60
crisp bean curd cubes 63
bean curd rolls with mushrooms 64
spring onion pancakes 66
crispy seaweed rolls 68
cabbage and bean curd patties 70
steamed minced meat dumplings 73
golden pouches 74
aubergine folders 76
mixed vegetable patties 78
weights and measures 80

chinese vegetarian

soup of dough slices Serves 4

Unlike handmade noodles where the dough has to be kneaded, rolled out and cut, this recipe simply requires that a batter be added to the boiling stock.

INGREDIENTS

Plain (all-purpose) flour	150 g (5 1/3 oz)
Salt	1/2 tsp
Egg	1
Dried Chinese mushrooms	3, soaked to soften, stems discarded and quartered
Wood ear and cloud ear fungus	55 g (2 oz), soaked to soften and sliced
Carrot	1, peeled and sliced
Chinese flowering cabbage (*choy sum*)	110 g (4 oz), cut into 5-cm (2-in) lengths

VEGETABLE STOCK

Cooking oil	2 Tbsp
White radish	1, peeled and sliced
Carrot	1, peeled and sliced
Onions	2, peeled and halved
Celery	4 stalks, cut into chunks
Fresh button mushrooms	55g (2 oz), halved
Water	3 litres (96 fl oz / 12 cups)
Salt	2 tsp
Bouquet garni (see Note)	
Black peppercorns	4

NOTE

Make a bouquet garni by tying together 2 sprigs of parsley, 1 sprig of thyme and 1 bay leaf. The vegetable stock can be kept refrigerated for 2–3 days or frozen for up to 1 month.

METHOD

- Prepare vegetable stock. Heat oil in a large pot and add all vegetables and mushrooms. Stir-fry for 5–7 minutes over medium heat, then add water, salt, bouquet garni and peppercorns. Bring to the boil, then lower heat to simmer for 30 minutes. Strain stock into a large pot and discard vegetables left in strainer.

- Sift flour with salt. Beat in egg and sufficient water to make a very thick batter. Let stand for 20 minutes, then beat again thoroughly.

- Place mushrooms, fungus, carrot and vegetables into a large pot with vegetable stock. Bring to the boil.

- Add spoonfuls of batter to boiling stock until batter is used up. Dough slices will form as batter is cooked. Lower heat and simmer for 5 minutes.

- Ladle into serving bowls and serve hot.

family pot Serves 4

Rich with ingredients, this dish is substantial enough to be served as a meal on its own.

INGREDIENTS

Dried bean curd skin	5 sheets, each 50 × 25-cm (20 × 10-in), soaked to soften and drained
Sichuan vegetable	110 g (4 oz), minced
Canned bamboo shoot	45 g (1½ oz), drained and finely sliced
Wonton wrappers	16 pieces
Cloud ear fungus	30 g (1 oz), soaked to soften, drained and finely sliced
Corn flour (cornstarch)	1 tsp, mixed with 2 tsp water
Ginger	0.5-cm (¼-in) slice
Vegetable stock (page 10)	1.25 litres (40 fl oz / 5 cups)
Carrot	1, peeled and cut into pieces
Dried Chinese mushrooms	8, soaked to soften, stems discarded
Water chestnuts	10, peeled, then blanched in boiling water for 2 minutes
Black moss	5 g (⅙ oz), soaked for 20 minutes and drained
Bean sprouts	55 g (2 oz), tailed

SEASONING

Salt	1½ Tbsp
Sugar	½ Tbsp
Light soy sauce	2 Tbsp

METHOD

- Shred 1 sheet of dried bean curd skin finely. Cut remaining 4 sheets into 1 x 5-cm (½ x 2-in) strips.

- Two different types of wonton are prepared for this dish. To make 8 wontons of the first type, mix half the Sichuan vegetable with finely shredded dried bean curd skin and bamboo shoot. Put 1 tsp filling on a wonton wrapper, bring edges of skin up to enclose filling and seal with corn flour mixture.

- To wrap 8 wontons of another filling, mix remaining Sichuan vegetable with cloud ear fungus. Put 1 tsp filling on each wonton wrapper, bring edges of skin up to enclose filling and seal with corn flour mixture.

- Place ginger and vegetable stock in a large pot and bring to the boil. Add carrot, mushrooms, water chestnuts, black moss and strips of dried bean curd skin. Return to the boil, then lower heat and simmer gently for 20 minutes.

- Add seasoning, wontons and bean sprouts. Return to the boil, then ladle into servings bowls and serve hot.

hot and sour soup Serves 4

This soup makes a good appetiser, with its slightly hot and sour flavour. Add more crunch to the soup with bean sprouts, if desired.

INGREDIENTS

Cooking oil	85 ml (2½ fl oz / ⅓ cup)
Dried Chinese mushrooms	4, soaked to soften, stems discarded and sliced
Soft bean curd	200 g (7 oz), cut into fine strips
Carrot	1, peeled and finely shredded
Salted vegetable	85 g (3 oz), soaked for 30 minutes, rinsed and finely sliced
Red chillies	3–4, washed and finely sliced
Black moss	5 g (⅙ oz), soaked for 20 minutes and drained
Enoki mushrooms	110 g (4 oz), root ends discarded
Vegetable stock (page 10)	1 litre (32 fl oz / 4 cups)
Corn flour (cornstarch)	2 Tbsp, mixed with 4 Tbsp water
Egg	1, lightly beaten

SEASONING A

Dark soy sauce	1 Tbsp
Salt	1½ tsp
Ground white pepper	½ tsp

SEASONING B

Malt vinegar	4 Tbsp
White vinegar	1 Tbsp
Sesame oil	2 tsp
Chopped coriander leaves (cilantro)	1 Tbsp

METHOD

- Heat oil in a wok and stir-fry Chinese mushrooms for 1 minute. Add all other shredded and sliced ingredients, black moss and enoki.

- Stir well, add vegetable stock and seasoning A. Bring to the boil, then lower heat and simmer for 2 minutes. Stir in corn flour mixture and return to the boil, stirring until soup thickens.

- Remove from heat and leave for 1 minute, then stir in beaten egg to cook in residual heat. Stir in seasoning B and serve immediately.

vegetarian shark's fin soup Serves 4

Cooked this way, glass noodles resemble glassy threads of cooked shark's fin, which is how this dish got its name.

INGREDIENTS

Cooking oil	4 Tbsp
Cloud ear and wood ear fungus	30 g (1 oz), soaked to soften and sliced
Glass noodles	55 g (2 oz), soaked to soften and drained
Dried Chinese mushrooms	4, soaked to soften, stems discarded and sliced
Chinese cabbage	100 g (3½ oz), finely sliced
Canned bamboo shoot	55 g (2 oz), drained and finely sliced
Carrot	100 g (3½ oz), peeled and shredded
Vegetable stock (page 10)	1 litre (32 fl oz / 4 cups)

SEASONING A

Salt	1½ tsp
Light soy sauce	1 Tbsp
Ground white pepper	½ tsp

SEASONING B

Corn flour (cornstarch)	1 Tbsp, mixed with 2 Tbsp water and 1 tsp sesame oil

METHOD

- Heat oil in a wok and stir-fry all ingredients together except stock and seasoning.

- Add seasoning A and stir-fry for 2 minutes. Add vegetable stock and bring to the boil.

- Stir in seasoning B and cook, stirring until mixture thickens slightly. Serve immediately.

pot of prosperity Serves 4

The fresh corn cobs serve not only to add flavour and sweetness to this mushroom and vegetable dish, but colour as well. Serve as part of a Chinese meal.

INGREDIENTS

Cooking oil	4 Tbsp
Onion	1, peeled and minced
Plain (all-purpose) flour	85 g (3 oz)
Vegetable stock (page 10)	1.625 litres (54 fl oz / 6½ cups)
Dried Chinese mushrooms	8, soaked to soften, stems discarded
Canned straw mushrooms	16, drained
Fresh button mushrooms	110 g (4 oz), caps wiped and stems discarded
Abalone mushrooms	6, caps wiped and stems discarded
Enoki mushrooms	110 g (4 oz), root ends discarded
Fresh corn	3 cobs, chopped into 2-cm (1-in) sections
Green peas	110 g (4 oz), blanched in hot water for 2 minutes and drained
Snow peas	55 g (2 oz), trimmed

SEASONING

Salt	2 tsp
Ground white pepper	½ tsp
Sugar	1 Tbsp
Minced ginger	½ tsp

METHOD

- Heat oil in a wok and stir-fry onion until lightly browned.

- Mix together flour and stock, adding liquid gradually while stirring to keep mixture smooth. Add to wok and bring to the boil over medium heat while stirring. Stir in seasoning.

- Add mushrooms and vegetables and bring to the boil. Ladle into serving bowls and serve hot.

soup of assorted shreds Serves 4

If the vegetable stock has already been pre-prepared, this dish takes just minutes to put together, making it ideal for a quick weekday meal.

INGREDIENTS

Dried bean curd skin	30 g (1 oz), soaked to soften, drained and finely sliced
Wood ear fungus	55 g (2 oz), soaked to soften, drained and finely sliced
Dried Chinese mushrooms	5–6, soaked to soften, stems discarded and finely sliced
Canned bamboo shoot	55 g (2 oz), drained and finely sliced
Vegetable stock (page 10)	1 litre (32 fl oz / 4 cups)

SEASONING

Salt	1 1/2 tsp
Ground white pepper	1/2 tsp

METHOD

- Place all sliced ingredients into a large heatproof bowl. Add seasoning and vegetable stock.
- Steam over gently boiling water for 40 minutes. Ladle into serving bowls and serve immediately.

shredded bean curd soup Serves 4

Compared to soft bean curd, pressed bean curd has a firm texture, and is flavoured with spices, among them five-spice powder, which gives it a yellow tinge.

INGREDIENTS

Baking soda	1 tsp
Yellow pressed bean curd	450 g (1 lb), cut into thin strips
Cooking oil	2 Tbsp
Dried Chinese mushrooms	4, soaked to soften, stems discarded and finely sliced
Canned bamboo shoot	55 g (2 oz), drained and finely sliced
Carrot	55 g (2 oz), peeled and shredded
Celery	55 g (2 oz), finely sliced
Straw mushrooms	55 g (2 oz)
Vegetable stock (page 10)	500 ml (16 fl oz / 2 cups)

SEASONING

Salt	$2/3$ tsp
Sesame oil	2 tsp

METHOD

- Bring a pot of water to the boil and add baking soda. Add bean curd strips and cook for 5 minutes, then drain and rinse under cold running water. Drain well and set aside.

- Heat oil in a wok and stir-fry Chinese mushrooms for 2 minutes. Add bamboo shoot, carrot, celery and straw mushrooms. Stir-fry for another 3 minutes.

- Add vegetable stock and seasoning. Bring to the boil and add bean curd strips. Return to the boil and cook for another 3 minutes. Ladle into serving bowls and serve immediately.

cucumbers with mung bean sheets Serves 6–8

This simple dish is quick-to-prepare and can be served with drinks at a cocktail party.

INGREDIENTS

Japanese cucumbers	3, ends trimmed
Garlic	4 cloves, peeled and minced
Salt	2 tsp
Sugar	2 Tbsp
Mung bean sheets	8 slices, soaked in cold water to soften and cut into 2-cm (1-in) wide strips
Toasted white sesame seeds	

SEASONING

Sesame oil	1 Tbsp
White vinegar	1 1/2 Tbsp

NOTE

If a spicy dish is preferred, substitute sesame oil with the same amount of chilli oil and add 2–3 chopped red chillies according to taste.

METHOD

- Crush cucumbers slightly with the flat of a cleaver. Halve them lengthwise, then cut into 2-cm (1-in) thick slices.

- Place cucumbers in a bowl with garlic, salt and sugar. Mix well, then cover with plastic wrap and refrigerate for at least 4 hours. The salt will help to draw out water from cucumbers.

- Remove cucumbers from refrigerator. Drain off excess water and toss with mung bean sheets.

- Stir in seasoning and sprinkle with toasted sesame seeds. Serve.

bean curd skin with black sesame seeds

Serves 4–6

This dish goes fabulously well with drinks. Prepare ahead and store in an airtight container.

INGREDIENTS

Cooking oil for deep-frying	
Dried bean curd skin	2 sheets, each 50 × 25-cm (20 × 10-in), cut into thin strips
Black sesame seeds	1 Tbsp

GARLIC SOY SAUCE

Light soy sauce	3 Tbsp
Minced garlic	1 Tbsp
Ground white pepper	1 Tbsp

METHOD

- Mix together all ingredients for garlic soy sauce. Store in a screw-cap jar.
- Heat oil for deep-frying until smoking hot. Lower strips of dried bean curd skin, a few at a time into hot oil, and deep-fry until golden brown and crisp. Remove and drain well.
- Drizzle garlic soy sauce over strips of fried bean curd skin. Sprinkle with black sesame seeds and serve.

simple fried rice Serves 4

Use day-old cooked rice if possible, as the grains tend to be drier and will not clump together when stir-fried. If using freshly cooked rice, allow rice to cool before stir-frying for best results.

INGREDIENTS

Cooked long-grain rice	450 g (1 lb)
Cooking oil	2 Tbsp
Eggs	4, lightly beaten
Spring onions (scallions)	6, finely sliced
Salt	1 tsp
Rice wine or dry sherry	$1/2$ tsp

METHOD

- Break up cooked rice grains with a pair of chopsticks or a fork.

- Heat oil in a wok. Add eggs and scramble lightly for 1 minute. Add rice and mix well.

- Stir in chopped spring onions and season with salt. Stir-fry for 3–4 minutes until eggs are cooked and rice grains are separate and dry.

- Stir in rice wine or sherry and cook for another 1 minute. Dish out and serve hot.

vegetarian glutinous rice Serves 6–8

Dried Chinese mushrooms add an appetising aroma to this simple rice dish, while giving it a lovely chewy texture that meat lovers will appreciate.

INGREDIENTS

White glutinous rice	450 g (1 lb)
Cooking oil	3 Tbsp
Shallots	6, peeled and finely chopped
Dried Chinese mushrooms	8, soaked to soften, stems discarded and finely sliced
Celery	2 stalks, finely chopped

SEASONING

Salt	1 tsp
Dark soy sauce	1 Tbsp
Ground white pepper	1/2 tsp
Vegetable stock (page 10)	85 ml (2 1/2 fl oz / 1/3 cup)
Rock sugar	10 g (1/3 oz)

METHOD

- Wash and drain rice. Place in a large pan of boiling water for about 10 minutes, making sure that rice is fully covered by water. Drain well and set aside.

- Heat oil in a wok and stir-fry shallots for 2 minutes, or until shallots are translucent. Add mushrooms, celery and seasoning. Stir-fry for 2 minutes, then add rice to wok and stir-fry over medium heat for 3 minutes, or until liquid evaporates.

- Transfer rice mixture into a heatproof bowl. Cover and steam over rapidly boiling water for 45 minutes, or until rice is tender and translucent.

- Remove from heat and serve hot. Garnish as desired.

stir-fried vermicelli   Serves 4

Cut the ingredients into thin strips of similar size for better presentation. This dish can be served as a meal on its own, or with other dishes for a more substantial meal.

INGREDIENTS

Cooking oil	90 ml (3 fl oz / 6 Tbsp)
Firm bean curd	1 piece, cut into small cubes
Red chillies	2, seeded and finely sliced
Dried Chinese mushrooms	6, soaked to soften, stems discarded and finely sliced
Carrot	1/2, peeled and finely shredded
Vegetable stock (page 10)	125 ml (4 fl oz / 1/2 cup)
Fine rice vermicelli	300 g (11 oz), soaked in warm water for 10 minutes and drained
Bean sprouts	100 g (3 1/2 oz)
Chopped Chinese chives	3 Tbsp

SEASONING

Light soy sauce	3 Tbsp
Salt	1 tsp
Ground white pepper	1/2 tsp
Sugar	1/2 tsp

METHOD

- Heat half the oil in a wok and deep-fry bean curd cubes until golden. Drain and set aside.

- Add remaining oil to wok and stir-fry red chillies for 5 seconds. Add Chinese mushrooms and stir-fry for 2 minutes. Add fried bean curd cubes, carrot, stock, vermicelli, bean sprouts and seasoning. Stir-fry over high heat for 5 minutes, or until vermicelli is almost dry.

- Add chopped chives and mix well. Serve immediately.

pekinese noodles in special sauce Serves 4–6

This vegetarian version of Pekinese noodles is flavoured with yellow bean sauce and vegetable stock, and is no less tasty compared to the traditional recipe which includes meat.

INGREDIENTS

Fresh egg noodles	500 g (1 lb 1½ oz)
Sesame oil	2 Tbsp
Cooking oil	4 Tbsp
Dried Chinese mushrooms	4, soaked to soften, stems discarded and diced
Yellow pressed bean curd	220 g (8 oz), cut into small cubes
Cucumber	½, small, finely shredded
Carrot	1, peeled and cut into small cubes
Canned bamboo shoot	85 g (3 oz), drained and cut into small cubes
Spring onions (scallions)	2, finely sliced

SEASONING

Yellow bean sauce	3 Tbsp
Dark soy sauce	½ Tbsp
Sugar	2 tsp
Vegetable stock	85 ml (2½ fl oz / ⅓ cup)

METHOD

- Bring a large pot of water to the boil. Add noodles and cook for 2 minutes, then drain well and place in a large serving bowl. Stir in sesame oil. Cover to keep noodles warm.

- Heat oil in a wok. Add mushrooms and bean curd and stir-fry for 2 minutes. Add seasoning and stir-fry for 1 minute. Add cucumber, carrot and bamboo shoot. Mix well and cook until sauce bubbles.

- Divide noodles among 4–6 serving bowls and ladle sauce over. Garnish with spring onions and serve hot.

fried mouse-tail noodles Serves 4–6

Unlike other noodles, mouse-tail noodles do not clump up when cold. As such it can be enjoyed freshly cooked, or at room temperature.

INGREDIENTS

Cooking oil for deep-frying	
Firm bean curd	2 pieces, each 220 g (8 oz), cut into small cubes
Mouse-tail noodles (*loh shee fun*)	600 g (1 lb 5⅓ oz)
Shallots	3, peeled and sliced
Garlic	3 cloves, peeled and finely minced
Dried Chinese mushrooms	5, soaked to soften, stems discarded and finely sliced
Carrot	1, peeled and shredded
Chinese flowering cabbage (*choy sum*)	2, cut into 2.5-cm (1-in) lengths
Bean sprouts	200 g (7 oz), tailed
Vegetable stock (page 10)	3 Tbsp
Spring onions (scallions)	2, chopped

SEASONING

Light soy sauce	1½ Tbsp
Dark soy sauce	1½ Tbsp
Sugar	½ tsp
Salt	½ tsp
Ground white pepper	¼ tsp

METHOD

- Heat oil in a wok and deep-fry bean curd until golden. Drain and set aside.

- Add 1 Tbsp oil to a pot of boiling water and scald noodles for 1 minute. Drain well and set aside.

- Heat 2 Tbsp oil in a wok and stir-fry shallots and garlic until lightly browned. Add mushrooms and carrot. Stir-fry for 2 minutes. Add fried bean curd, Chinese flowering cabbage and bean sprouts. Toss briefly.

- Add seasoning and scalded noodles. Continue to stir-fry for 2–3 minutes. Stir in vegetable stock and fry until noodles are dry.

- Dish out and garnish with spring onions. Serve.

shanghainese fried rice cakes Serves 4

Also known as new year cake or *nian gao,* Shanghainese rice cakes are made of glutinous rice flour and have a lovely chewy texture when cooked.

INGREDIENTS

Cooking oil	3 Tbsp
Dried Chinese mushrooms	10, soaked to soften, stems discarded and halved
Dried Shanghai rice cakes (*nian gao*)	300 g (11 oz), soaked overnight to soften, drained
Chinese cabbage	280 g (10 oz), cut into 2.5-cm (1-in) sections
Sesame oil	1 tsp
Spring onion (scallion)	1, sliced

SEASONING

Light soy sauce	1 1/2 Tbsp
Dark soy sauce	1 Tbsp
Sugar	1/4 Tbsp
Salt	1/2 tsp
Vegetable stock (page 10)	125 ml (4 fl oz / 1/2 cup)

METHOD

- Heat oil in a wok. Add mushrooms and stir-fry for 2 minutes, then add seasoning. Cover wok and simmer for about 2 minutes.

- Add rice cakes and Chinese cabbage. Stir-fry for 5 minutes, or until vegetables are tender and ingredients are well-mixed.

- Dish out and sprinkle sesame oil over. Garnish with spring onion and serve hot.

golden mushrooms with grated ginger Serves 4–6

Lightly flavoured with sherry and grated ginger, this mushroom dish is simple yet tasty. Serve as part of a Chinese meal.

INGREDIENTS

Fresh button mushrooms	450 g (1 lb)
Cooking oil	125 ml (4 fl oz / $1/2$ cup)
Light soy sauce	2 Tbsp
Grated ginger	$1/2$ Tbsp
Corn flour (cornstarch)	1 Tbsp, mixed with 2 Tbsp water
Spring onion (scallion)	1, chopped

SEASONING

Salt	$2/3$ tsp
Sugar	1 Tbsp
Ground white pepper	$1/3$ tsp
Vegetable stock (page 10)	85 ml ($2 1/2$ fl oz / $1/3$ cup)
Sherry	$1/2$ tsp

METHOD

- Wash mushrooms in water mixed with a little salt. Trim off and discard stalks. Pat dry with paper towels, then make shallow cuts on caps.

- Heat oil in a wok and fry mushrooms until golden. Remove with a slotted spoon, then soak in light soy sauce for 20 minutes.

- Leave 1 Tbsp oil in wok and stir-fry grated ginger for 1 minute. Add fried mushrooms and seasoning and stir-fry for a few minutes.

- Add corn flour mixture to thicken sauce. Dish out and garnish with spring onion. Serve.

stuffed chinese mushrooms Serves 4–6

Water chestnuts add crunch, while salted vegetables lend a unique salty flavour to this pretty dish of stuffed mushrooms.

INGREDIENTS

Dried Chinese mushrooms	16–20, large, soaked to soften, stems discarded
Corn flour (cornstarch)	1 Tbsp
Soft bean curd	300 g (11 oz)
Water chestnuts	5, peeled and minced
Carrot	1, small, peeled and minced
Salted vegetable	30 g (1 oz), soaked in water for 30 minutes, drained and minced
Cooking oil	2 Tbsp
Green peas	16–20, blanched in hot water for 2 minutes

SEASONING

Ground white pepper	$1/2$ tsp
Salt	$1/2$ tsp
Sugar	$1/2$ tsp
Corn flour (cornstarch)	1 Tbsp

SAUCE

Cooking oil	$1/2$ Tbsp
Light soy sauce	$1 1/2$ Tbsp
Sugar	1 tsp
Water	3 Tbsp
Salt	$1/3$ tsp
Corn flour (cornstarch)	1 Tbsp, mixed with 2 Tbsp water

METHOD

- Coat inner sides of mushroom caps with corn flour and set aside.

- Mash bean curd and mix with water chestnuts, carrot, salted cabbage and seasoning to make stuffing for mushrooms.

- Heat oil in a wok and stir-fry stuffing for 2 minutes. Remove from wok with a slotted spoon. Leave to cool slightly.

- Divide stuffing among mushrooms, pressing mixture firmly into caps. Press a green pea firmly on top of each stuffed mushroom. Place on a steaming plate and steam, covered, over rapidly boiling water for 15–20 minutes.

- Prepare sauce. Heat oil in a wok and add soy sauce, sugar and water. Bring to the boil, then stir in corn flour mixture to thicken. Pour sauce over steamed mushrooms and serve hot.

chinese mushrooms with braised chestnuts

Serves 4–6

Chestnuts are sweet and have a smooth texture, and add both taste and texture to this simple braised dish.

INGREDIENTS

Dried Chinese mushrooms	16
Dried chestnuts	450 g (1 lb), soaked overnight

SEASONING

Dark soy sauce	3 Tbsp
Rock sugar	30 g (1 oz)
Salt	$1/3$ tsp
Liquorice root	7–8 slices
Sesame oil	2 tsp

NOTE
If liquorice root is not available, replace with an equal quantity of mint leaves.

METHOD

- Soak mushrooms in 600 ml (20 fl oz / 2½ cups) hot water for 20 minutes. Remove mushrooms and discard stems. Place soaking liquid in a pot.

- Drain and wash soaked chestnuts under cold running water. Add to pot with mushrooms and seasoning.

- Bring water to the boil, then lower heat and simmer, covered, for about 1 hour, or until nearly all liquid has been absorbed and chestnuts are tender. Check pot occasionally and add more water, if necessary, to prevent ingredients from burning.

- Dish out and serve immediately.

abalone mushrooms in sweet-sour sauce
Serves 4

With their meaty texture, abalone mushrooms make a perfect substitute for meat. Here, they are deep-fried and coated in a mouth-watering sweet-sour sauce.

INGREDIENTS

Abalone mushrooms	250 g (9 oz)
Salt	½ tsp
Five-spice powder	¼ tsp
Corn flour (cornstarch)	130 g (4½ oz)
Rice flour	130 g (4½ oz)
Self-raising flour	130 g (4½ oz)
Cooking oil	625 ml (20 fl oz / 2½ cups)
Garlic	1 clove, peeled and chopped
Tomato	½, cut into cubes
Cucumber	¼, cut into cubes
Green capsicum (bell pepper)	½, cut into cubes
Pineapple	85 g (3 oz), cut into cubes
Corn flour (cornstarch)	1 Tbsp, mixed with 1 Tbsp water

SAUCE

Tomato sauce	5 Tbsp
Chilli sauce	2½ Tbsp
Salt	to taste
Sugar	1 Tbsp
White vinegar	2 Tbsp
Water	180 ml (6 fl oz / ¾ cup)

METHOD

- Marinate abalone mushrooms with salt and five-spice powder. Set aside for 20 minutes.

- Mix corn flour, rice flour and self-raising flour in a large bowl. Coat mushrooms thoroughly and set aside.

- Heat oil and deep-fry mushrooms over high heat until golden brown. Drain well and set aside. Reserve 1 Tbsp oil.

- Reheat oil in a clean wok and add garlic, tomato, cucumber, green capsicum and pineapple. Stir-fry lightly, then add combined ingredients for sauce. Bring to the boil and stir in corn flour mixture to thicken sauce.

- Allow sauce to return to the boil, then add fried mushrooms and mix well. Serve hot.

vegetables with bean curd knots Serves 4

The Cantonese name for black moss is *fat choy*, which sounds like the Cantonese word for "prosperity". As such, black moss is a popular ingredient used in Chinese New Year dishes.

INGREDIENTS

Cooking oil	2 Tbsp
Minced spring onion (scallion)	1 Tbsp
Dried bean curd knots (see Note)	110 g (4 oz)
Baking soda	1/4 tsp
Vegetable stock (page 10)	125 ml (4 fl oz / 1/2 cup)
Canned straw mushrooms	10, drained and halved
Black moss	5 g (1/6 oz), soaked for 10 minutes and drained
Carrot	1, peeled and cut into cubes
Corn flour (cornstarch)	1 Tbsp, mixed with 2 Tbsp water

SEASONING

Salt	1 tsp
Sugar	1 tsp
Ground white pepper	1/2 tsp

NOTE

To make bean curd knots, soak bean curd sheets in cold water until soft. Pat dry and cut into 8 x 2-cm (3 x 1-in) strips. Tie into knots and soak in cold water for another 5 minutes before use. Ready-made dried bean curd knots are available from Chinese grocery stores and some supermarkets. Soak to soften before use.

METHOD

- Heat oil in a wok and stir-fry spring onion until it begins to brown. Add bean curd knots, baking soda and vegetable stock. Bring to the boil and leave boiling for 3 minutes.

- Add seasoning, straw mushrooms, black moss and carrot. Cook for another 2 minutes, then stir in corn flour mixture to thicken sauce. Dish out and serve.

water chestnuts in black bean sauce Serves 4

Water chestnuts retain their lovely crunchy texture even after cooking, as is evident in this dish.

INGREDIENTS

Cooking oil	4 Tbsp
Water chestnuts	350 g (12 oz), peeled and washed
Fermented black beans	2 Tbsp, soaked for 10 minutes, rinsed and drained
Minced garlic	1/2 Tbsp
Green peas	30 g (1 oz), blanched in hot water for 2 minutes
Water	2 Tbsp

SEASONING

Salt	1/2 tsp
Sugar	1/2 tsp
Ground white pepper	1 tsp

METHOD

- Heat oil and stir-fry water chestnuts for 2 minutes. Remove with a slotted spoon. Reserve 1 Tbsp oil in frying pan.

- Stir-fry fermented black beans and garlic until garlic turns brown. Add green peas and water. Stir-fry for another minute.

- Combine stir-fried ingredients with water chestnuts in a heatproof bowl. Cover and steam over rapidly boiling water for 20 minutes. Toss with seasoning.

- Dish out and serve.

bean cake strips with french beans Serves 4

In place of the usual mock meats, this recipe uses a healthier alternative—green bean flour patties, which can be quickly and easily prepared.

INGREDIENTS

Green (mung) bean flour	125 g (4½ oz)
Rice flour	70 g (2½ oz)
Water	
Cooking oil	
Chilli powder	⅔ tsp
French beans	8–10, trimmed and sliced
Wood ear fungus	55 g (2 oz), washed, drained and finely sliced
Carrot	½, peeled and shredded
Bean sprouts	55 g (2 oz), tailed
Vegetable stock (page 10)	4 Tbsp

SEASONING

Salt	1 tsp
Dark soy sauce	1 Tbsp

METHOD

- Mix green bean flour and rice flour with sufficient water to form a thick batter the consistency of heavy cream.

- Heat 1 Tbsp oil in a frying pan. Ladle about 3 Tbsp batter into pan to form a pancake about 10-cm (4-in) in diameter. Fry on both sides over medium heat until lightly browned. Continue making more pancakes until batter is used up. Cut pancakes into fine strips.

- Heat 2 Tbsp oil in a wok and stir-fry chilli powder for 30 seconds. Add French beans, fungus, carrot and bean sprouts. Stir-fry for 2 minutes.

- Add pancake strips, seasoning and vegetable stock. Cover and simmer for 1–2 minutes. Dish out and serve.

stuffed cucumber Serves 4

These stuffed cucumbers make a pretty party dish.

INGREDIENTS

Cucumber	1, large
Corn flour (cornstarch)	1 Tbsp
Soft bean curd	300 g (11 oz), mashed
Dried Chinese mushrooms	6, soaked to soften, stems discarded and minced
Water chestnuts	45 g (1½ oz), peeled and minced
Carrot	1, small, peeled and minced
Salted vegetable	30 g (1 oz), soaked in water for 30 minutes, washed and minced
Cooking oil	75 ml (2½ fl oz / 5 Tbsp)
Vegetable stock (page 10)	180 ml (6 fl oz / ¾ cup)
Sesame oil	1½ tsp

SEASONING A

Salt	⅔ tsp
Dry mustard	½ tsp
Corn flour (cornstarch)	1 Tbsp
Egg white	1

SEASONING B

Salt	1 tsp
Ground white pepper	½ tsp

METHOD

- Peel cucumber and trim off ends. Cut into 2.5-cm (1-in) thick rounds and use a small round cutter to cut out the soft centres. Wash cucumber rings and pat dry with paper towels. Dust inside of rings with corn flour.

- Mix mashed bean curd with all minced ingredients and seasoning A. Mix well. Heat 2 Tbsp oil and stir-fry mixture for 2 minutes. Pack into cucumber rings.

- Heat remaining oil in a frying pan and lightly cook stuffed cucumber rings over medium heat until just browned.

- Pour vegetable stock over cucumber rings and bring to the boil. Lower heat and simmer very gently for 20 minutes until cucumbers are tender. Add seasoning B and sesame oil. Transfer to a deep serving dish and serve hot.

stuffed bitter gourd Serves 4

Bitter gourd is rich in essential vitamins and minerals. Consuming the gourd is also believed to help increase the body's resistance to infection, among other health benefits.

INGREDIENTS

Bitter gourds	2
Corn flour (cornstarch)	1 Tbsp
Firm bean curd	2 pieces, each 220 g (8 oz)
Water chestnuts	85 g (3 oz), peeled and minced
Dried Chinese mushrooms	4, soaked to soften, stems discarded and minced
Cooking oil	4 Tbsp
Green peas	30 g (1 oz), blanched in hot water for 2 minutes and drained

SEASONING A

Salt	1/2 tsp
Corn flour (cornstarch)	1 Tbsp
Sesame oil	1/2 Tbsp
Five-spice powder	1/3 tsp
Sugar	1/2 tsp

SEASONING B

Light soy sauce	1 1/2 Tbsp
Vegetable stock (page 10)	3 Tbsp
Minced garlic	1/2 Tbsp
Fermented black beans	1 Tbsp, soaked for 10 minutes, rinsed and drained
Sugar	1 Tbsp
Salt	1/2 tsp

METHOD

- Trim ends of bitter gourds and cut into 2.5-cm (1-in) thick rings. Scoop out seeds and discard. Place bitter gourd rings in a large pan of water. Bring to the boil for 2 minutes, then drain well. Pat gourd rings dry, then dust insides of rings with corn flour. Set aside.

- Blanch bean curd in boiling water for 3 minutes. Drain and pat dry with paper towels. Cut off and discard hard outer layer. Mash remainder and mix with minced water chestnuts and Chinese mushrooms. Stir in seasoning A.

- Heat 3 Tbsp oil in a wok and stir-fry mashed bean curd mixture for 1–2 minutes. Remove from wok with a slotted spoon and press into bitter gourd rings. Place rings on a steaming plate, cover and steam over boiling water for 15–20 minutes until bitter gourd is tender.

- Heat remaining oil in a wok. Stir-fry green peas with seasoning B for 1 minute. Spoon over steamed bitter gourd rings and serve hot.

bean curd strips with chinese chives Serves 4–6

Serve this simple stir-fry of pressed bean curd and Chinese chives as part of a Chinese meal, with freshly steamed white rice.

INGREDIENTS

Cooking oil	2 Tbsp
Yellow pressed bean curd	2 pieces, each 220 g (8 oz), cut into 1 × 2.5-cm ($1/2$ × 1-in) pieces
Vegetable stock (page 10)	85 ml ($2^1/2$ fl oz / $1/3$ cup)
Chinese chives	1 bunch, washed and cut into 2.5-cm (1-in) sections

SEASONING

Salt	1 tsp
Sugar	$1^1/2$ tsp
Light soy sauce	$1/2$ Tbsp
Ground white pepper	$1/2$ tsp

METHOD

- Heat oil in a wok and stir-fry pressed bean curd for 2–3 minutes. Add vegetable stock and seasoning and stir-fry over gentle heat for 5–7 minutes, until liquid is reduced.

- Add chives and stir-fry for another 1–2 minutes. Dish out and serve immediately.

bean curd rolls with basil Serves 6

Simply stuffed with basil and deep-fried, these crisp and fragrant bean curd rolls are fun as a snack and make pretty party food.

INGREDIENTS

Dried bean curd skin	10 sheets, each 25 × 15-cm (10 × 6-in), soaked for 3 minutes to soften
Basil leaves	70 g (2½ oz), chopped
Plain (all-purpose) flour	2 Tbsp, mixed with 1½ Tbsp water
Cooking oil for deep-frying	

SEASONING

Light soy sauce	2 tsp
Sugar	2 tsp
Ground white pepper	½ tsp

METHOD

- Pat bean curd skin dry with paper towels, taking care not to break or tear them. Set 6 sheets aside and chop remaining 4 sheets finely. Squeeze out any excess moisture.

- Mix chopped bean curd skin with chopped basil leaves and add seasoning.

- Place a sheet of bean curd skin on top of another. Spoon one-third of basil mixture in a line onto one long side of bean curd sheets. Roll bean curd skin up to enclose filling, then seal with flour paste. Leave sides of each roll exposed.

- Repeat step above to make 2 more rolls with remaining sheets of bean curd skin and basil mixture.

- Heat oil and deep-fry rolls for about 5 minutes. Remove and drain well. Leave to cool before cutting into sections. Serve.

crisp bean curd cubes Serves 2–3

Covered with a light and crisp skin, these bean curd cubes are melt-in-your mouth delicious! Serve with the dip recipe provided, or your favourite sweet chilli sauce.

INGREDIENTS

Soft bean curd	300 g (11 oz), cut into 4-cm (1½-in) cubes
Cooking oil for deep-frying	
Egg	1, lightly beaten
Plain (all-purpose) flour	180 g (6½ oz)
Spring onion (scallion)	1, finely sliced

DIP

Light soy sauce	3 Tbsp
Garlic	1 clove, peeled and minced
Sugar	½ tsp
Sesame oil	2 tsp

METHOD

- Place bean curd cubes in a bowl and scald with boiling water for 1 minute. Drain well on paper towels.

- Heat oil in a wok.

- Dip bean curd cubes into beaten egg, then coat lightly with flour. Deep-fry coated bean curd cubes a few at a time for 3–4 minutes until golden. Remove with a slotted spoon and drain well. Arrange on a serving plate.

- Mix ingredients for dip together in a small bowl.

- Garnish bean curd cubes with spring onion and serve with dip.

bean curd rolls with mushrooms Serves 4–6

The steamed bean curd sheets take on a soft and melting texture. This simple yet tasty dish goes well with plain porridge or white rice.

INGREDIENTS

Dried bean curd skin	16 sheets, each 25 x 15-cm (10 x 6-in), soaked for 3 minutes to soften
Cooking oil	1 Tbsp
Dried Chinese mushrooms	4, soaked to soften, stems discarded and finely sliced

SAUCE

Vegetable stock (page 10)	300 ml (10 fl oz / 1¼ cups)
Light soy sauce	2 Tbsp
Rock sugar	30 g (1 oz)
Liquorice root	8 slices
Cinnamon	1 stick

SEASONING

Light soy sauce	4 Tbsp
Sugar	2½ Tbsp
Five-spice powder	1 tsp
Salt	½ tsp
Sesame oil	1 Tbsp

METHOD

- Pat bean curd skins dry with paper towels, being careful not to tear them.

- Heat oil in a wok and add combined seasoning ingredients and sliced mushrooms. Stir-fry for 3 minutes. Set aside.

- Place ingredients for sauce in a pot and bring to the boil. Lower heat and simmer for 20 minutes. Discard cinnamon and set sauce aside.

- Lay a sheet of bean curd skin on a flat work surface. Spread a thin layer of mushrooms over, then place another bean curd skin over. Repeat layering 8 times, then roll bean curd skins up. Repeat with remaining ingredients to make another roll.

- Wrap bean curd rolls in muslin and tie with string to secure. Steam over simmering water for 25 minutes. Remove and cool slightly, then remove string and muslin. Slice bean curd rolls and serve with sauce.

spring onion pancakes Makes 4

Fragrant with the aroma of spring onions, these crisp Chinese pancakes can be enjoyed on their own or as an accompaniment to rice porridge.

INGREDIENTS

Spring onions (scallions)	6, finely sliced
Salt	1 tsp
Cooking oil	4 Tbsp

SCALDED DOUGH

Plain (all-purpose) flour	300 g (11 oz)
Boiling water	300 ml (10 fl oz / 1¼ cups)

METHOD

- Prepare scalded dough. Sift flour into a mixing bowl. Add boiling water gradually while stirring continuously to mix well. Cover bowl with a damp cloth and let stand for about 10 minutes.
- Knead mixture into a rough dough. Add more flour or water, if necessary. Dough should feel damp but not wet. Cover with a damp cloth and let stand for another 20 minutes.
- Knead dough vigorously by pushing and pulling it apart. Finish off by kneading dough for about 15–20 minutes until dough is smooth.
- Divide dough into 4 and roll each piece to 0.5-cm (¼-in) thickness. Brush with a little oil, then sprinkle with spring onions and salt. Roll dough into a ball, then flatten into a round about 12-cm (5-in) in diameter.
- Heat oil in a pan and fry pancakes over medium heat until golden brown on both sides. Drain well and serve hot.

crispy seaweed rolls Serves 4

Lightly frying the seaweed rolls gives them a wonderful crisp texture.

INGREDIENTS

Carrot	1, peeled and cut into long, thin strips
Cucumber	$1/2$, peeled and cut into long, thin strips
Canned bamboo shoot	55 g (2 oz), drained and cut into long, thin strips
Wood ear fungus	55 g (2 oz), soaked to soften and finely sliced
Salt	$1/2$ tsp
Nori (seaweed)	3 sheets
Plain (all-purpose) flour	2 Tbsp, mixed with $1 1/2$ Tbsp water
Cooking oil	2 Tbsp

DIP

Light soy sauce	3 Tbsp
Water	3 Tbsp
Corn flour (cornstarch)	2 tsp
Chilli powder	$1/2$ tsp

METHOD

- Place carrot, cucumber, bamboo shoot and wood ear fungus in a colander and sprinkle with salt.

- Lay nori sheets on a flat working surface and arrange an equal portion of vegetables, bamboo shoot and wood ear fungus on each sheet. Roll up and seal ends with flour paste.

- Prepare dip. Combine dip ingredients in a small saucepan. Stir well and bring to the boil. Remove from heat and set aside to cool.

- Heat oil in a frying pan and pan-fry seaweed rolls over medium heat for 5 minutes, turning them constantly.

- Remove and slice thickly. Serve with dip on the side.

cabbage and bean curd patties Makes 8

These cabbage and bean curd patties can be enjoyed on their own or dipped into chilli sauce.

INGREDIENTS

Chinese cabbage	450 g (1 lb)
Salt	2 tsp
Soft bean curd	300 g (11 oz), drained and mashed
Dried Chinese mushrooms	5, soaked to soften, stems discarded and minced
Cooking oil	90 ml (3 fl oz / 6 Tbsp)
Scalded dough (page 66)	

SEASONING

Light soy sauce	1/2 Tbsp
Sugar	1/2 Tbsp
Ground white pepper	1 tsp
Corn flour (cornstarch)	1 Tbsp
Sesame oil	1/2 Tbsp

METHOD

- Rub cabbage with salt and leave for 10 minutes. Wash salt off cabbage and gently squeeze out excess water using hands. Chop finely. Mix mashed bean curd with cabbage, mushrooms and seasoning.

- Prepare scalded dough. Divide into 8 portions.

- Roll each portion into a ball, then flatten into rounds about 6-cm (2 1/2-in) in diameter. Spoon 1–2 Tbsp cabbage mixture onto the centre of each round, then enclose. Roll dough into a ball, then flatten using a rolling pin.

- Heat oil and pan-fry patties for about 10 minutes on each side or until lightly golden. Drain well and serve hot.

steamed minced meat dumplings Makes 12

Sichuan vegetable wih its salty flavour and crunchy texture adds both taste and texture to this dim sum dish.

INGREDIENTS

Cooking oil	2 Tbsp
Sichuan vegetable	70 g ($2^1/_2$ oz), soaked in water for 30 minutes, drained and minced
Minced meat	150 g ($5^1/_3$ oz), drained and minced
Scalded dough (page 66)	1 quantity, or 12 wonton wrappers

SEASONING

Sugar	$^1/_2$ Tbsp
Light soy sauce	$^1/_2$ tsp
Ground white pepper	$^1/_2$ tsp
Water	4 Tbsp

METHOD

- Heat oil in a wok and stir-fry Sichuan vegetable and minced meat for 2 minutes, breaking meat up. Add seasoning and mix well. Cover and cook for another 2 minutes, then set aside to cool.

- If using scalded dough, knead dough until smooth, then shape into a long roll. Cut into 12 equal sections, then roll each section into a thin round. Alternatively, use round wonton wrappers and omit this step.

- Spoon 2 tsp Sichuan vegetable and meat mixture onto the centre of each dough round or wonton wrapper. Fold over into semi-circles and pinch the edges of the dough around filling to seal.

- Line a steamer with a sheet of damp muslin, then arrange dumplings on top. Cover and steam over rapidly boiling water for 8–10 minutes. Serve immediately.

golden pouches Makes 10

These attractive little deep-fried pouches can also be served as finger food. Serve with a sweet chilli sauce for dipping, if desired.

INGREDIENTS

Cooking oil	4 Tbsp + more for deep-frying
Garlic	4 cloves, peeled and finely chopped
Soft bean curd	200 g (7 oz), finely diced
Water chestnuts	6, peeled and minced
Carrots	200 g (7 oz), peeled and minced
Dried Chinese mushrooms	6, soaked to soften, stems discarded and finely sliced
Glass noodles	55 g (2 oz), soaked in hot water to soften and drained
Spring onions (scallions)	2, finely chopped + 10, blanched for 2 minutes
Corn flour (cornstarch)	1 tsp, mixed with 1 Tbsp water
Spring roll wrappers	10, each 10-cm (4-in) square

SEASONING

Oyster sauce	2 Tbsp
Light soy sauce	1 tsp
Ground white pepper	$1/2$ tsp
Sesame oil	$1/2$ tsp

METHOD

- Heat 4 Tbsp oil in a wok and stir-fry garlic, bean curd, water chestnuts, carrots and mushrooms until lightly fragrant. Mix in seasoning.

- Cut glass noodles into short strands, then add to wok with chopped spring onions. Mix well. Stir in corn flour mixture and cook until sauce is thick. Set aside to cool before using as filling.

- Lay a sheet of spring roll wrapper on a work surface. Spoon 4 tsp filling in the centre, then bring edges of spring roll wrapper together to form a pouch, enclosing filling. Secure pouch with a length of blanched spring onion. Trim pouch top with scissors. Repeat until all ingredients are used up.

- Heat oil for deep-frying and deep-fry pouches until golden brown. Remove with a slotted spoon and drain well. Serve hot.

aubergine folders Makes about 30

A treat for aubergine lovers. Coating the aubergines in batter before cooking helps them retain their shape.

INGREDIENTS

Firm bean curd	220 g (8 oz)
Black moss	5 g ($^1/_6$ oz), soaked in cold water for 20 minutes and drained
Long purple aubergines (eggplants/brinjals)	4, each about 16-cm (6$^1/_2$-in) long
Plain (all-purpose flour)	120 g (4$^1/_2$ oz)
Salt	$^1/_2$ tsp
Eggs	2, lightly beaten
Cooking oil	1 Tbsp + more for deep-frying
Water	

SEASONING

Salt	$^1/_2$ tsp
Ground white pepper	$^1/_2$ tsp
Egg white	1

SAUCE

Oyster sauce	3 Tbsp
Water	1$^1/_2$ Tbsp
Salt	$^1/_2$ tsp
Spring onion (scallion)	1, minced
Garlic	2 cloves, peeled and finely minced
Cooking oil	1 Tbsp

METHOD

- Blanch bean curd in boiling water for 3 minutes. Drain and pat dry. Cut off and discard hard outer layer and mash remainder. Mix well with black moss and seasoning. Set aside.

- Wash aubergines and discard ends. Cut into 2-cm (1-in) thick slices, then cut in between each slice, almost through, to make 'folders'. Press 1/2 Tbsp bean curd mixture into each 'folder'.

- Mix flour with salt in a bowl. Make a well in the centre and add beaten eggs and 1 Tbsp oil. Gradually stir flour into eggs, adding sufficient water to make a smooth batter the consistency of heavy cream. Let batter stand for 10 minutes.

- Mix all ingredients for sauce together except oil. Heat oil and add sauce to cook for 2–3 minutes. Set aside.

- Heat cooking oil for deep-frying. Coat aubergine folders with batter and deep-fry for about 4 minutes each, until puffed up and golden brown. Remove with a slotted spoon and drain well. Serve with sauce.

mixed vegetable patties Makes 6

The combination of wood ear fungus, dried lily buds, Sichuan vegetable and water chestnuts all add a delightful crunchy texture to these mixed vegetable patties.

INGREDIENTS

Soft bean curd	300 g (11 oz), drained and mashed
Wood ear fungus	15 g (1/2 oz), soaked to soften and finely sliced
Dried lily buds	30 g (1 oz), soaked for 30 minutes, drained and roughly chopped
Sichuan vegetable	45 g (1 1/2 oz), soaked in water for 20 minutes, drained and finely sliced
Onion	1, small, peeled and minced
Water chestnuts	85 g (3 oz), peeled and minced
Spring onion (scallion)	1, finely minced
Cooking oil	150 ml (5 fl oz / 10 Tbsp)

SEASONING A

Corn flour (cornstarch)	2 Tbsp
Salt	1/2 tsp
Ground white pepper	1/2 tsp

SEASONING B

Light soy sauce	1 1/2 Tbsp
Water	3 Tbsp
Sugar	1/2 Tbsp

METHOD

- Combine all ingredients except spring onion, oil and seasoning in a bowl and mix well. Add seasoning A and mix well.

- Heat 2 Tbsp oil in a wok and stir-fry mixture for 2 minutes. Remove and set aside. When cool, divide mixture into 6 portions and form into flat, round patties.

- Heat 100 ml (3 1/2 fl oz) oil in a frying pan and cook patties until golden brown on both sides. Dish out.

- Heat remaining oil in a clean frying pan and add seasoning B. Bring to the boil, then pour over patties. Serve immediately.

weights and measures

Quantities for this book are given in Metric, Imperial and American (spoon and cup) measures. Standard spoon and cup measurements used are: 1 tsp = 5 ml, 1 Tbsp = 15 ml, 1 cup = 250 ml. All measures are level unless otherwise stated.

Liquid And Volume Measures

Metric	Imperial	American
5 ml	1/6 fl oz	1 teaspoon
10 ml	1/3 fl oz	1 dessertspoon
15 ml	1/2 fl oz	1 tablespoon
60 ml	2 fl oz	1/4 cup (4 tablespoons)
85 ml	2 1/2 fl oz	1/3 cup
90 ml	3 fl oz	3/8 cup (6 tablespoons)
125 ml	4 fl oz	1/2 cup
180 ml	6 fl oz	3/4 cup
250 ml	8 fl oz	1 cup
300 ml	10 fl oz (1/2 pint)	1 1/4 cups
375 ml	12 fl oz	1 1/2 cups
435 ml	14 fl oz	1 3/4 cups
500 ml	16 fl oz	2 cups
625 ml	20 fl oz (1 pint)	2 1/2 cups
750 ml	24 fl oz (1 1/5 pints)	3 cups
1 litre	32 fl oz (1 3/5 pints)	4 cups
1.25 litres	40 fl oz (2 pints)	5 cups
1.5 litres	48 fl oz (2 2/5 pints)	6 cups
2.5 litres	80 fl oz (4 pints)	10 cups

Dry Measures

Metric	Imperial
30 grams	1 ounce
45 grams	1 1/2 ounces
55 grams	2 ounces
70 grams	2 1/2 ounces
85 grams	3 ounces
100 grams	3 1/2 ounces
110 grams	4 ounces
125 grams	4 1/2 ounces
140 grams	5 ounces
280 grams	10 ounces
450 grams	16 ounces (1 pound)
500 grams	1 pound, 1 1/2 ounces
700 grams	1 1/2 pounds
800 grams	1 3/4 pounds
1 kilogram	2 pounds, 3 ounces
1.5 kilograms	3 pounds, 4 1/2 ounces
2 kilograms	4 pounds, 6 ounces

Length

Metric	Imperial
0.5 cm	1/4 inch
1 cm	1/2 inch
1.5 cm	3/4 inch
2.5 cm	1 inch

Oven Temperature

	°C	°F	Gas Regulo
Very slow	120	250	1
Slow	150	300	2
Moderately slow	160	325	3
Moderate	180	350	4
Moderately hot	190/200	375/400	5/6
Hot	210/220	410/425	6/7
Very hot	230	450	8
Super hot	250/290	475/550	9/10

Abbreviation

tsp	teaspoon
Tbsp	tablespoon
g	gram
kg	kilogram
ml	millilitre